Ralph Vaughan Williams
Songs of Travel

To access companion recorded accompaniments online, visit:
www.halleonard.com/mylibrary

Enter Code
7150-3417-9262-7313

BOOSEY & HAWKES

AN **IMAGEM** COMPANY

DISTRIBUTED BY

HAL•LEONARD®
CORPORATION
7777 W. BLUEMOUND RD. P.O. BOX 13819 MILWAUKEE, WI 53213

www.boosey.com
www.halleonard.com

PREFACE

Ralph Vaughan Williams (1872–1958) composed art songs which are among the best British works in the genre, particularly in the first decade of the twentieth century. He composed a few art songs before 1900, but his earliest noteworthy song is "Linden Lea," composed in 1901. In the same year Vaughan Williams composed "Whither must I wander," which would become part of *Songs of Travel*. The remaining songs in the cycle, originally for baritone and piano, were composed in 1904. His 1903 song cycle *The House of Life*, which includes the perennial favorite "Silent Noon," is also from the same period. Other major works for voice from this early period in the composer's work are *A Sea Symphony* (composed 1903–09), and *On Wenlock Edge* (composed 1908–09). Vaughan Williams achieved wide and varied success in other genres, particularly with orchestral and choral pieces. He returned to song composition in the 1920s, producing 21 songs in that decade. The composer turned again to writing art songs in the 1950s. Vaughan Williams also made quite a few arrangements of English folksongs for voice and piano.

The first eight songs in *Songs of Travel* were first performed as a "complete" set in London in 1904. The ninth song, "I have trod the upward and downward slope" was discovered in the composer's manuscripts after his death by his widow, Ursula Vaughan Williams, and added in 1960 to the first complete edition of the cycle. The citation was added to the added song's publication: "This little epilogue to the Song Cycle *Songs of Travel* should be sung in public only when the whole cycle is performed."

The composer orchestrated "The Vagabond," "The Roadside Fire" and "Bright is the ring of words." British composer Roy Douglas, musical assistant to Vaughan Williams at one time, later orchestrated the remaining songs of the cycle, employing the same instrumentation used by Vaughan Williams.

The Scottish writer Robert Louis Stevenson (1850–94) is best remembered for his novels *Treasure Island*, *Kidnapped*, and the novella *The Strange Case of Dr. Jekyll and Mr. Hyde*. He enjoyed a celebrated reputation as an unconventional adventurer, and traveled widely in his short life in Europe and the United States before settling in Samoa. (He died there at a young age from a probable cerebral hemorrhage.) Stevenson was also a sometime composer and arranger, and set some of his poems to music himself. The poetry collection *Songs of Travel and Other Verses* was published posthumously in 1896. The following editor's note appeared in the original edition:

> The following collection of verses, written at various times and places, principally after the author's final departure from England in 1887, was sent home by him for publication some months before his death. He had tried them in several different orders and under several different titles, as "Songs and Notes of Travel," "Posthumous Poems," etc., and in the end left their naming and arrangement to the present editor…

There are 44 poems in Stevenson's *Songs of Travel and Other Verses*. From these Ralph Vaughan Williams chose nine. Stevenson's title for the poem used in the first song of the cycle is "The Vagabond (To an air of Schubert)." It is not known what Schubert song Stevenson had in mind. The song title "The Roadside Fire" is Vaughan Williams' (the poem appears without a title).

—Richard Walters

CONTENTS

Pianist on the Recording: Laura Ward

The price of this publication includes access to companion recorded accompaniments online,
for download or streaming, using the unique code found on the title page.
Visit www.halleonard.com/mylibrary and enter the access code.

The Vagabond

original key

ROBERT LOUIS STEVENSON

RALPH VAUGHAN WILLIAMS

Allegro moderato
(alla marcia)

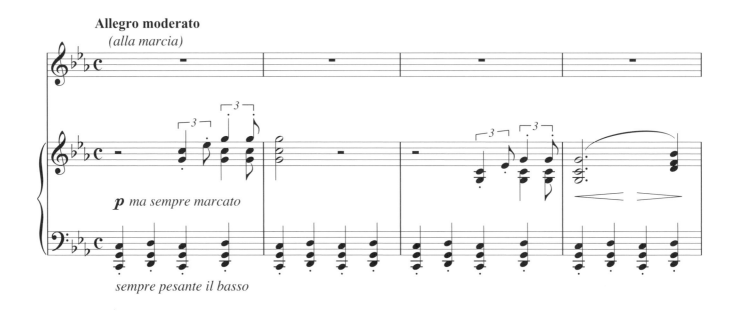

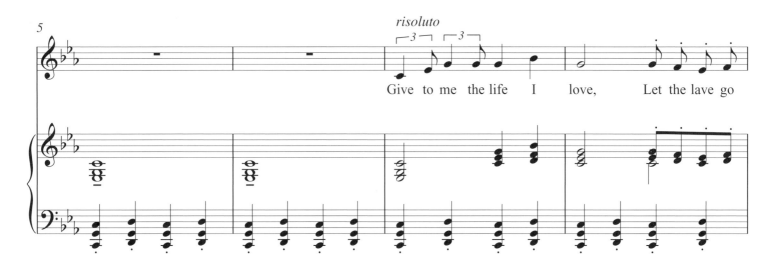

Give to me the life I love, Let the lave go by me, Give the jol-ly heaven a - bove, And the by-way nigh me.

o'er   me;   Give the face of earth a - round,   And the road be - fore   me.

Wealth   I seek not, hope   nor love,   Nor a ___ friend to   know

me;   All   I   seek,   the heaven a - bove, _____ And the

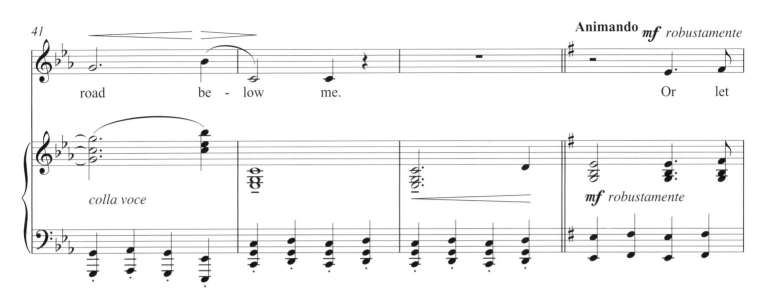

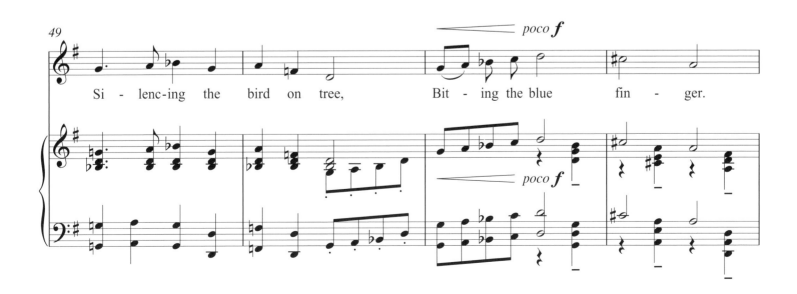

White as meal the fros-ty field— Warm the fire-side ha - ven—

Not to au-tumn will I yield, Not to win - ter e - ven!

Let the blow fall soon or late, Let what will be o'er me; Give the face of earth a -

Let Beauty awake
original key

ROBERT LOUIS STEVENSON

RALPH VAUGHAN WILLIAMS

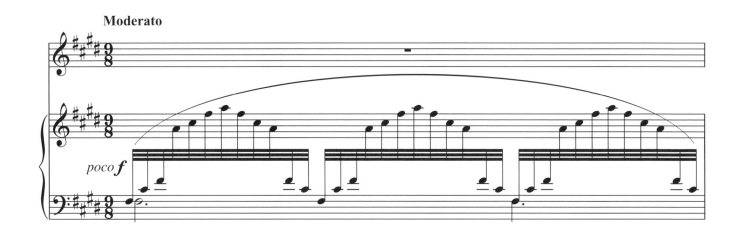

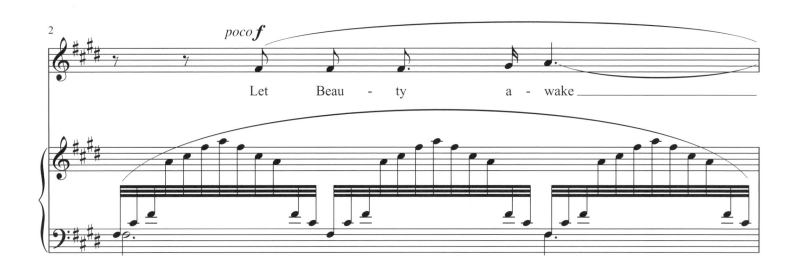

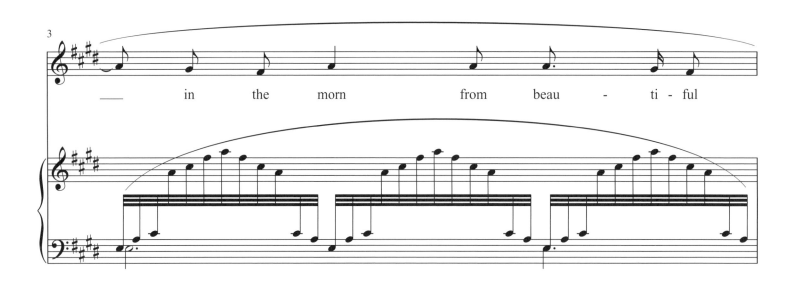

dreams, Beau - ty a - wake from

rest! Let Beau - ty a - wake For Beau - ty's

sake In the hour when the birds a - wake in the

brake And the stars are bright in the west!

cend, _____ Let her wake to the kiss of a ten - der friend, To

ren - der a - gain _____ and re - ceive!

The Roadside Fire
original key

ROBERT LOUIS STEVENSON

RALPH VAUGHAN WILLIAMS

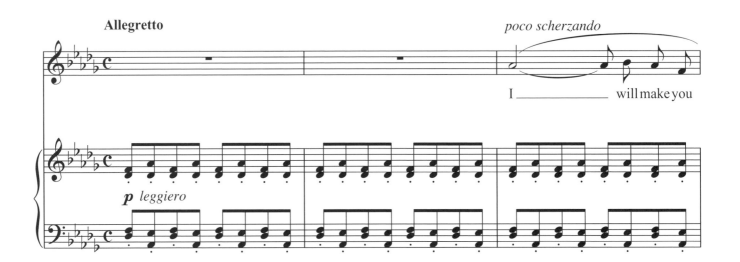

I _____ will make you

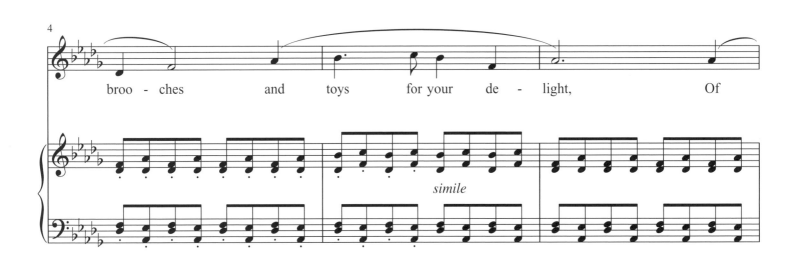

broo - ches and toys for your de - light, Of

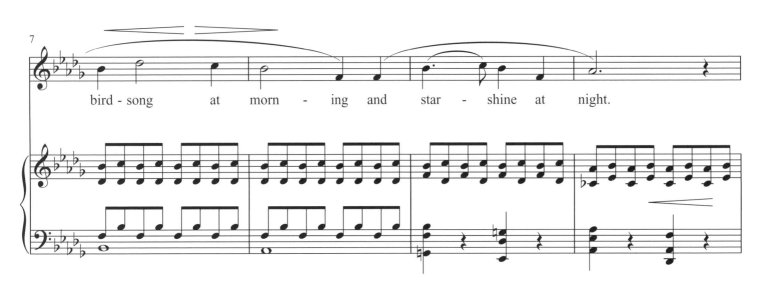

bird - song at morn - ing and star - shine at night.

ri - ver and bright blows the broom; And you _____ shall wash your

lin - en, and keep your bo - dy white In rain - fall at

morn - ing and dew - fall at night.

And

rall - en - tan - do

Youth and Love

original key

ROBERT LOUIS STEVENSON

RALPH VAUGHAN WILLIAMS

In dreams

original key

ROBERT LOUIS STEVENSON

RALPH VAUGHAN WILLIAMS

The infinite shining heavens
original key

ROBERT LOUIS STEVENSON

RALPH VAUGHAN WILLIAMS

*In Stevenson's original poem this word is 'stood'.

Whither must I wander?

original key

ROBERT LOUIS STEVENSON

RALPH VAUGHAN WILLIAMS

Home no more home to me, whi-ther must I wan - der? Hun - ger my dri - ver, I go where I must.

Cold blows the win-ter wind o-ver hill and hea - ther: Thick drives the

rain and my roof is in the dust. Lov'd of__ wise men was the

shade of my roof - tree, The true word of wel - come was spo - ken in the door:—

Dear days of old__ with the fa - ces in the fire - light; Kind folks of

old, you__ come a - gain no more.

Bright is the ring of words

original key

ROBERT LOUIS STEVENSON

RALPH VAUGHAN WILLIAMS

And when the west is red With the
sun - set em - - - bers,
The lov - er lin - gers and
sings, And the maid re - mem - - bers.

I have trod the upward and the downward slope

original key

ROBERT LOUIS STEVENSON

RALPH VAUGHAN WILLIAMS

This little epilogue to the Song Cycle *Songs of Travel* should be sung in public only when the whole cycle is performed.